# NEO-WORDS

**A Dictionary of the Newest and
Most Unusual Words of Our Times**

# NEO-WORDS

## A DICTIONARY OF THE NEWEST AND MOST UNUSUAL WORDS OF OUR TIMES

## DAVID K. BARNHART

**Illustrated by Elwood H. Smith**

**Collier Books / Macmillan Publishing Company**
**New York**
**Collier Macmillan Canada**
**Toronto**
**Maxwell Macmillan International**
**New York · Oxford · Singapore · Sydney**

To my wife, Hollis,
and my son, William

Collier Books
Macmillan Publishing Company
866 Third Avenue, New York, NY 10022

Collier Macmillan Canada, Inc.
1200 Eglinton Avenue East, Suite 200
Don Mills, Ontario M3C 3N1

Library of Congress Cataloging-in-Publication Data
Barnhart, David K.
    Neo-words: a dictionary of the newest and most unusual
words of our times /David K. Barnhart.—1st Collier Books ed.
        p.    cm.
    ISBN 0-02-028225-7
    1. English language—New words—Dictionaries.
    2. English language—Terms and phrases. I. Title.
PE1630.B26  1991                    90-42238  CIP
423'.1—dc20

Macmillan books are available at special discounts for bulk purchases for
sales promotions, premiums, fund-raising, or educational use. For details,
contact:

        Special Sales Director
        Macmillan Publishing Company
        866 Third Avenue
        New York, NY 10022

First Collier Books Edition 1991

10   9   8   7   6   5   4   3   2   1

Printed in the United States of America

# To the Reader:

This little book provides but a glimpse at some of the more unusual and colorful new words that have become popular in recent years. I have purposely favored such unusual neologisms as AIR BOUNCE, BATHUB CURVE, and CALIFORNIA BLACK TIE over the familiar neologisms so often cited as the litmus of our age, such as *AIDS* (in medicine), *black hole* (in science), *crack* (for cocaine), *hacker* (in computers), *network with* (in business), and *rap* (in music). The list of candidates is enormous.

Over the past decade I have worked with my father, Clarence L. Barnhart, on a journal to update dictionaries with new words (such as AEROBICIZE and CELEBUTANTE), new meanings for established vocabulary (such as BITCHIN' and JELLIES), and changes in English usage (such as the verb use of UZI and the appearance of A-THON as a freestanding form). These and the other entries in this book are gleaned from *The Barnhart DICTIONARY COMPANION*—a quarterly journal that each year records 1,500 words and meanings which cannot yet be found in either general or new-words dictionaries.

The growth of the English language is often lamented, sometimes vehemently, as a fact of LANGUAGE POLLUTION. Certainly, some new expressions are less attractive or less elegant than one might desire. But as Professor Victor Golla of Georgetown University has aptly pointed out, "The creative act that doesn't respond to some kind of social need isn't going to be picked up." For as long as scientists probe the frontiers of nature, musicians experiment with sound, clothing designers juggle the dictates of fashion, and teenagers seek evermore outlandish expressions to describe their experiences, the language *will* grow. Sometimes the growth will resemble weeds, other times flowers.

Harry Homa, a teacher of English at Morris High School in the Bronx, New York, begins the study of dictionary skills by pointing out to his students that "some words fly, others die." And so it will be with the entries presented in this book. Those words which fill a hole in our vocabulary will fly for as long as the need for them persists. The need has, perhaps, expired for *break dancing, Cabbage Patch doll, Fosbury flop, hoola hoop, sky marshal,* and *yellow rain,* for they are far less often seen or heard than in the past.

Some terms come into currency as the need arises, only to fall out of fashion until once again revived; *gunboat diplomacy* is attested from the 19th century, being revived when tensions in the diplomatic world become inflamed.

Words which fall from use sometimes will leave some legacy. *Watergate* spawned the combining form *-gate* as seen in the surfeit of relatively unimportant terms, such as *cookiegate, Briefing-gate, gospelgate, Pageantgate, sewergate, winegate,* and many more. They are unimportant except that they share *-gate,* denoting "a scandal often involving a cover-up scheme." *Abscam,* in a similar way, popularized the use of *-scam* as a combining form. GRIDLOCK has flourished, however, and given us the combining form -LOCK.

Some novelties will survive so well that they lose the aura of newness. Among these are *ombudsman* (1960s), *exit poll* (1970s), and *joint venture* (1960s).

So furious is the current pace of change in English that keeping up with new words and new meanings is beyond the scope of any single research program. However, all lexicographers who deal with new words are going to be watching the events in Europe— both economic and political; *Communism* will need to be redefined soon.

Thomas Jefferson noted our need to allow language to adapt to our ever-changing worlds; in a letter dated August 16, 1813, he advised the author of a new grammar:

Yet I have no hesitation in saying that the English language is . . . capable, with the like freedom of employing its materials, of becoming superior to [French] in copiousness and euphony. Not indeed by holding fast to Johnson's Dictionary; not by raising a hue and cry against every word he has not licensed; but by encouraging and welcoming new compositions of its elements. . . . Its enlargement must be the consequence, to a certain degree, of its transplantation from the latitude of London into every climate of the globe; and the greater the degree the more precious will it become as the organ of the development of the human mind.

We must not allow our established linguistic habits to become a tyranny of linguistic propriety; nor ought we to embrace neologisms only on account of their freshness.

No book is the product of a single person; this book is no exception. The idea to produce a popular book of recent "real words" based upon the material in *The Barnhart DICTIONARY COMPANION* was that of my first editor at Macmillan, John Glusman. His idea was prompted by Richard Bernstein's article in *The New York Times* about my work. That article is directly attributable to Professor Allan Metcalf, a colleague and friend. Thanks go also to Robert Kimzey, Philip Turner, and finally to Nancy Cooperman, who shepherded the production at Macmillan.

Special thanks I extend to Charlotte R. Morrill, Cecile Lindstedt, and especially Gail Greet Hannah for encouraging me to look at my work from a new perspective. And to Elwood Smith, my deep appreciation for his artistic insights.

I am indebted, of course, to my father, Clarence L. Barnhart, whose ideas spawned *The Barnhart DICTIONARY COMPANION.*

I am particularly grateful to my wife, Hollis, who deserves much credit for helping me over the trials of writing, revising, and waiting for the project to be completed. Thanks go, too, to my son, William, that years from now he may know that he provided moments of merriment when sharing occupancy in the "dictionary pit."

Such errors of fact and opinion as, no doubt, reside within these pages are mine alone. I invite the reader to communicate facts and opinions so that I may more widely cast the net of lexicographic inquiry into the sea of our language.

—David K. Barnhart
Cold Spring, N.Y.
July 11, 1990

**access charge**

## abortuary

*n.* An abortion clinic. This term is used by critics of legalized abortion to place a stigma of evil upon such places.

Recorded from 1984 (on the *MacNeil/Lehrer News-Hour*). Constructed by joining *abortion* (as in *abortion clinic*) with *mortuary*. The rhyme of the Latin roots cleverly emphasizes the message of the antiabortion activist Joseph M. Scheidler, the director of the Pro-Life Action League of Chicago, who popularized the term.

## access charge

*n. phr.* The fee that a long-distance telephone company pays to a local telephone company for the expense of initiating and completing long-distance calls.

Recorded from 1985 (in the *Legal Times*). Constructed by combining *access* (as in *access road* or *access time*) with *charge* (as in *carrying charge* or *service charge*).

## aeroback

*n.* An automobile design in which the rear portion slopes down from the roof to the bumper less evenly than the continuous line of a fastback, but more evenly than the line of a notchback.

Recorded from 1982 (in the *Sunday Times Magazine,* published in London). Constructed by joining *aero-* (as in *aerodynamic)* with *-back* (as in *fastback, hatchback,* and *notchback).*

## aerobicize

*v.* To follow a program of exercises designed to increase the body's efficient use of oxygen in order to achieve and maintain good physical condition.

Recorded from 1981 (in *The Dial,* published by WNET-TV). Constructed by joining *aerobic* (as in *aerobic dancing)* with the suffix *-ize.* Other new words with *-ize* include: *alimonize, Carterize, genderize, hamburgerize, Lebanonize,* and *museumize.*

## air-bounce

*v.* To throw a Frisbee or similar disk so that it dips and then rises abruptly in flight without touching the ground.

Recorded from 1984 (in *The New Yorker*). Constructed by joining *air* (as in *air drop*) with *bounce,* because of the similarity with a ball that bounces on a floor, as in a bounce pass in basketball.

## air guitar

*n.* An imaginary guitar played with the body movements of a rock musician, often as an amusing accompaniment to recorded music.

Recorded from 1982 (in *The New York Times*). Constructed by combining *air* (as in *air curtain*) with *guitar* (as in *electric guitar*).

## aliterate

*n.* A person who prefers watching television and movies or listening to radio to reading a book or magazine.

Recorded from 1966 (in *The Washington Post*). Constructed by substituting the prefix *a-* (as in *amoral*) for the prefix *il-*, meaning "not," in *illiterate*. The adjective form, *a-literate*, is recorded from 1966 (in *Saturday Review*).

**aliterate**

### anorexia athletica

*n.* Great loss of appetite by a young woman as the result of such excessive physical training that normal bodily functions are disrupted.

Recorded from 1987 (in *Muscle & Fitness* magazine). Constructed by combining *anorexia* (in the medical term *anorexia nervosa*) with the made-up word *athletica* (from *athletic*, as if it were a Latin word with the suffix -*a*).

### Arablish

*n.* The Arabic language laced with many words from English in the same way that French, Hindi, Japanese, and Spanish have borrowed so many English words that they have been dubbed Fringlish, Hinglish, Japlish, and Spanglish.

Recorded from 1984 (in *The Johannesburg Star*). Constructed by joining the clipped form of *Arabic* with -*lish* (as in *English*). The letter *l* is included to avoid ambiguity with other language names ending in -*ish*.

### a-thon

*n.* long-lasting event in which participants seek to raise funds for a charitable group.

Recorded from 1983 (in *The Christian Science Monitor*). Constructed by treating the popular combining form *-athon* or *-a-thon* (found to form so many new words, such as *bikeathon, dance-a-thon, phone-a-thon,* and *walkathon*) as an independent word.

## barbecue mode

*n. phr.* A maneuver that slowly rotates a space-craft in order to distribute the sun's heat evenly over the craft's surface.

Recorded from 1977 (in *Aviation Week and Space Technology* magazine). Constructed by combining *barbecue* (as in *barbecue spit*) with *mode* (as in *landing mode, approach mode,* or *cruise mode* in the jargon of airplane pilots).

## bathtub curve

*n.* A curve on a graph that shows an early period with a steep rate of change followed by a long period of little or no change followed by another period with a steep rate of similar change.

Recorded from 1983 (in *Production Engineering* magazine). Constructed by combining *bathtub*, because the curve resembles the cross section of a

**bathtub curve**

bathtub, with *curve* (as in *bell curve* or *Laffer curve*).

## Beijing Spring

*n. phr.* Also called **Peking Spring.** A brief time in the early summer of 1989 when Chinese students and workers demonstrated in Tiananmen Square in Beijing for the greater freedom associated with Western-style democracies.

Recorded from 1989 (in *Time* magazine). Constructed by combining *Beijing* (or *Peking*), with *spring*, patterned after *Prague Spring* from the late 1960s and early 1970s.

## binuclear family

*n. phr.* A family in which legal separation or divorce of a married couple with children creates two households.

Recorded from 1981 (in *Science 81* magazine). Constructed by joining the prefix *bi-*, meaning "two," with the phrase *nuclear family,* meaning "basic family unit."

## biochip

*n.* A computer chip that relies on the biological function of proteins and enzymes to send signals rather than on the flow of electrons, theoretically producing faster computers, often called *biocomputers.*

Recorded from 1982 (in *Computerworld* magazine). Constructed by joining the combining form *bio-*, meaning "life," with *chip* (as in *silicon chip*), meaning "an integrated circuit in a computer etched on a small piece of silicon."

## bitchin'

*adj.* **1.** very good, excellent.
**2.** fashionable, groovy, cool, with it.

Recorded from 1979 (in *The Washington Post*). Constructed as a variant of *bitching* from the verb *bitch*, meaning "grumble" or "complain." The wrenching of meaning is the same kind of reversal exhibited by the word *bad*, as in "He's a bad dude," when the word really is used to mean "good."

## blipvert

*n.* Any advertisement that has been greatly compressed from many seconds to just a few seconds while containing the same amount of information.

Recorded from 1985. Constructed by joining *blip,* meaning "the speck on a radar screen," with the clipped form of *advert,* itself a clipping of *advertisement.* Coined by the originators of the character Max Headroom, a TV journalist who investigates cases of viewers who explode from information overload, in the TV movie *Max Headroom: 20 Minutes into the Future.*

## blush wine

*n. phr.* A category of wine with a pink color paler than rose, made from red grapes, thought to have originated in the Sonoma Valley of California.

Recorded from 1985 (in *The New York Times Magazine).* Constructed by combining the clipped form of *blush-rose,* the term describing a pink rose flower, with *wine* (as in *white wine*).

## boardsailing

*n.* Also known by the older term *windsurfing.* The sport of riding a surfboard equipped with a mast and sail. **Boardsailors** first competed in the Olympic Games in 1984.

Recorded from 1980 (in *The Washington Post).* Constructed by joining the clipped form of the word *surfboard* with the term *sailing* (as in *skate sailing*).

*Windsurfing* is the older term, having appeared in print about 1970.

## boom car

*n. phr.* An automobile with a very loud radio or cassette player intended to be heard by people outside of the car.

Recorded from 1989 (in the *Los Angeles Times*). Constructed by combining *boom* (box) with *car* (as in *touring car* or *sports car*). This term is not related to *boom car,* meaning "a railroad car with a crane."

## bourgeois liberalization

*n. phr.* The adoption of Western political values when they conflict with traditional Communist policy. A term used by conservative Chinese politicians who are trying to slur the reputation of those seeking a change in policy.

Recorded from 1986 (in the *Japan Economic Journal*). Probably a loan translation from a Chinese term.

## boutique farmer

*n. phr.* A person who specializes in the raising of exotic fruits, vegetables, or other agricultural

**boom car**

produce for gourmet restaurants and retail shops in urban markets.

Recorded from 1980 (in *The Washington Post*). Constructed by combining *boutique,* meaning "a shop for trendy clothes," with *farmer* (as in *truck farmer* or *dairy farmer*).

## bright collar

*adj.* Young, well-educated, and professional, especially when associated with the computer field.
*n.* A professional worker who is young and well educated, especially in the computer field.

Recorded from 1985 (in *The New York Times*). Constructed by substituting *bright,* meaning "shining, intelligent, quick-witted," for the first word in the group of compounds: *blue collar, white collar, gray collar, pink collar, new collar,* and *rainbow collar,* where *collar* refers to a shirt color representing some level of skill or other attribute of a worker.

## Butterfly Effect

*n. phr.* The major impact resulting from a minor force left unchecked over a long time, such as the multiplying of a draft from a butterfly's wing in Beijing to a hurricane in Washington, D.C. See also CHAOS THEORY.

Recorded from 1984 (1979?). Constructed by combining *butterfly,* because the shape of a computer graph resembles the outspread wings of a butterfly, with *effect* (as in *ripple effect).* Dr. Edward N. Lorenz first presented the image in a paper in 1979; before that he had used the image of a sea gull's wing to illustrate the effect.


## California black tie

*n. phr.* An unconventionally colorful variation of a tuxedo, often with the trousers shortened in the style of Bermuda shorts, colorful knee socks, running shoes, or creative substitutes for bow ties.

Recorded from 1989. Constructed by combining *California* (as in *California roll,* a sushi roll with colorful ingredients) with *black tie,* the informal term for a tuxedo. Reported to have been the invention of Ms. Winter Horton, a screenwriter in Hollywood.


## camo

*n.* **1.** A color combination and pattern resembling the camouflage garments of soldiers and their equipment.
**2.** A shirt, pen, or other item with such a pattern, as a fad in fashion.

Recorded from 1980 (in *The Washington Post*). A clipping of *camouflage,* a term borrowed from French.

## celebutante

*n.* A person who is a new and popular subject of gossip in fashionable society.

Recorded from 1985 (in *Forbes* magazine). Constructed by clipping *celebrity* and blending it with a clipped form of *debutante.*

## chaos theory

*n. phr.* The systematic approach to describing very complex events in mathematics and science by rounding off numerical data to reveal very general patterns, as in describing the irregular patterns of a dripping water faucet, fluctuations in insect populations, and stock market price changes.

Recorded from 1984 (in popular literature in *High Technology* magazine). Constructed by combining *chaos,* "nature subject to no law," with *theory* (as in *number theory* or *probability theory*).

## chaotic attractor

*n. phr.* Also called **strange attractor.** A pattern of movement in a system with motion, such as a dripping water faucet or a flock of birds, which is very complex and changeable.

Recorded from 1986 (in popular literature in *The Christian Science Monitor*). (*Strange attractor* from 1976.) Constructed by combining *chaotic* (as in *chaotic anarchy*) with *attractor,* because the pattern of movement seems to be drawn to a certain complex repetitive state.

*Strange attractor* has been attributed to the inventiveness of the French scientists David Ruelle and Floris Takens, which would suggest that the term may derive from a translation of French, perhaps *attracteur étrange* or *attracteur bizarre.*

## circlevision

*n.* The showing of a movie on a screen which completely surrounds the viewers.

Recorded from 1980 (in *The New York Times Magazine*). Constructed by combining *circle* (as in *circle dance*) with *-vision* (as in *Vistavision* or *Panavision*).

## cocktail diplomacy

*n. phr.* Verbal persuasion and discussion rather than warfare, terrorism, or other forceful tactics of international political procedure.

**cocktail diplomacy**

Recorded from 1983 (in *The Economist*). Constructed by combining *cocktail* (as in *cocktail party*) with *diplomacy* (as in *gunboat diplomacy* or *dollar diplomacy*).

## colorize

*v.* To tint a black-and-white motion picture, especially a very old one, to make it more marketable. The reaction of many people prompted the appearance of the word **decolorize,** meaning "to change a colorized film to its former black-and-white form."

Recorded from 1984 (in *Time* magazine). Constructed by joining *color* (as in *color print)* with the suffix *-ize* (as in *verbalize*). This is an invention independent of the technical use in metallurgy.

## computer widow

*n.* A woman whose husband is preoccupied with working on a computer, especially in place of paying attention to her. The equality of the sexes has prompted the appearance of the parallel term **computer widower**.

Recorded from 1982 (in *Byte* magazine). Constructed by combining *computer* (as in *computer data*) with *widow* (as in *war widow* or *golf widow)*.

### croissantisation

*n.* The popularization of croissants as a part of people's diet in a trendy society. See also JUNK-FOOD IMPERIALISM.

Recorded from 1984 (in *The New Yorker*). Constructed by joining *croissant*, meaning "the French roll recently made popular with a wide variety of fillings," with the suffix *-ization*, because evidence of *croissantize* is lacking.

### cyberphilia

*n.* The mental outlook of someone who is unusually fascinated with using computers. See also COMPUTER WIDOW.

Recorded from 1982 (in *Computerworld* magazine). Constructed by joining *cyber-*, a combining form meaning "computerization" (as in *cybernetics*), with *-philia,* the combining form meaning "love of or liking for _____." This word may have been formed by substituting *-philia* for the second element in the earlier term *cyberphobia*.

### cyberphobia

*n.* Also called **computerphobia**. The mental outlook of someone who is intimidated to an unusual degree by the power and complexity of computers.

cyberphilia

Recorded from 1981 (in *Discover* magazine). Constructed by joining *cyber-* (as in *cybernetics* or *cybernation*) with *-phobia*, the combining form meaning "fear, hatred, or dread of _____" (as in *technophobia* or *cancerphobia).*

## dead-man rule

*n. phr.* A strategy in criminal law which suggests that an accused person should seek to shift the blame to someone who is dead and consequently cannot testify in his own defense.

Recorded from 1987 (in *The New Yorker*). Constructed by combining *dead-man* (compare *dead-man's pinch*, an unexplainable bruise) with *rule* (as in *ground rule*[s]).

## death star

*n.* Also called **Nemesis**. A companion star to the Sun that some people suggest causes periodic meteor showers creating mass extinctions on Earth.

Recorded from 1984 (in *Discover*). Constructed by combining *death* (as in *death ray*) with *star* (as in *cannibal star* or *neutron star*).

**death star**

## designer genes

*n. pl.* Genetic material that has been altered through genetic engineering for use in agricultural and medical experiments.

Recorded from 1980 (in *The New York Times*). Constructed as a pun on *designer jeans,* by combining *designer,* meaning "created by a high-fashion clothing designer," with *gene* (as in *artificial gene* or *cancer gene*).

## diaper drama

*n. phr.* A theatrical play in which the plot focuses upon the problems encountered by young and middle-aged adults learning to get along successfully with their own parents. Also called **diaper play.**

Recorded from 1984 (in *The New York Times*). Constructed by combining *diaper* with *drama* (as in *folk drama* or *tank drama*). The use of *diaper* suggests that the parents still have some control over the children. The term *diaper play* was first found by my research staff in *The New Republic* in 1986.

## DINK

*n.* Either member of a couple with no children to support, each of whom has an income.

Recorded from 1987 (in *The Washington Post*). Constructed as an acronym from the phrase *d*ouble *i*ncome *no* *k*ids. The word arose from the yuppie culture of North America and has given rise to many, mostly humorous and short-lived, acronyms, such as:

*sink*—single income no kids

*SIBIM*—single income but I moonlight

*nilok*—no income, lots of kids

*sibihalf*—single income but I have a live-in friend.

### docutainment

*n.* Also called **infotainment.** A videotape or motion picture based upon fact and presented in an entertaining way.

Recorded from 1983 (in *The Washington Post*). Constructed by joining the clipped form of *documentary* (as in *docudrama*) with the clipped form of *entertainment* (as in *containment, detainment, ascertainment,* etc., in which *-tain-* comes from Latin *tenere* "to hold").

### dumb down

*v. phr.* To make textbooks easier to understand by reducing the reading level of the text.

**dumb down**

Recorded from 1980 (in an interview with James Michener in *U.S. News & World Report*). Constructed by combining *dumb*, the adjective used as a verb, with *down* (as in the verb phrases *build down* and *run down*). *Dumb* as a verb is recorded only in the meaning "to make or become silent."

## ear candy

*n.* Popular music which is easy to listen to because it is soft and pleasing.

Recorded from 1984 (in *Time* magazine). Constructed by combining *ear* (as in *tin ear*) with *candy*, meaning "something pleasing" (as in the expression *sugar-candy hymns* or *sugar-candy terms*).

## eater-out

*n., pl.* **eaters-out** or **eater-outs**. A person who frequents restaurants rather than dining at home.

Recorded from 1980 (in *Forbes* magazine). Probably constructed irregularly by combining *eat out*, the verb phrase, with the suffix *-er*, meaning "one who _____."

## EFTPOS

*n.* The payment for a purchase by the computerized transfer of money between bank accounts at the time and place the purchase is made.

Recorded from 1985 (in *The Economist*). Constructed by combining *EFT*, an acronym standing for "electronic funds transfer," with *POS*, another acronym standing for "point of sale."

## electropollution

*n.* Excessive amounts of electromagnetic waves in the environment due to the increasingly widespread use of electricity and the electrical and electronic equipment it powers.

Recorded from 1986 (in *Vogue* magazine). Constructed by combining *electro-* (as in *electroshock*) with *pollution* (as in *noise pollution*).

## Eurotunnel

*n.* A consortium of British and French firms that seeks to construct a tunnel under the English Channel to accommodate high-speed rail traffic.

Recorded from 1980 (in *The Economist*). Constructed by joining the combining form *Euro-* (as in *Europort, Eurobank*, and *Eurocurrency)* with *tunnel* (as in *drainage tunnel*). The earlier term *chunnel*, a

**electropollution**

combination of *channel* and *tunnel,* has a definitely sarcastic connotation.

## faddict

*n.* A person who compulsively follows a temporary fashion. This condition has been described as a **faddiction.**

Recorded from 1987 (in *Time* magazine). Constructed by blending *fad* with *addict* (as in *drug addict*).

## fax hacker

*n. phr.* A person who uses a fax machine to send messages that have not been requested by the recipient, usually in large numbers or to many people.

Recorded from 1989 (in *The New York Times*). Constructed by combining *fax* (as in *fax machine*) with *hacker,* meaning "a computer hobbyist who seeks to gain unauthorized access to a computer data base through a telephone connection for purposes of making mischief."

## flexiplace

*n.* A place at home set aside for working that is connected by computer to an office, thereby

**flightseeing**

enabling the worker to avoid commuting to an office. Also called **electronic cottage,** which allows for *telecommuting.*

Recorded from 1983 (in *Computerworld Extra!*). Constructed by joining the combining form *flexi-,* meaning "flexible" (as in *flexitime*), with the clipped form of *workplace.*

## flightseeing

*n.* Sightseeing done by airplane or helicopter rather than by automobile, bus, or foot.

Recorded from 1981 (in *The Christian Science Monitor*). Constructed by joining *flight* (as in *charter flight*) with the clipped form of *sightseeing.*

## floor hockey

*n.* A game resembling field hockey, played on a gymnasium floor with a puck and hockey sticks, often with fewer players than are found on field hockey teams.

Recorded from 1978 (in *The Washington Post*). Constructed by combining *floor* (as in *floor exercises*) with *hockey* (as in *ice hockey, knock hockey,* etc.).

## gender-bender

*n.* A person, style, or object which by its nature obscures sex differences, especially in fashion design or language.

Recorded from 1980 (in *The Economist*). Constructed by combining *gender*, meaning "sex," with *bender*, meaning "one who stretches or distorts something from its normal appearance" (as in *mindbender*).

## gender-crossing

*adj.* For the opposite sex, especially having to do with clothing for one sex but designed in the style customarily associated with the opposite sex, such as men's style of underwear marketed to women.

Recorded from 1983 (in *Women's Wear Daily*). Constructed by combining *gender*, meaning "sex," with *crossing*, meaning "opposite" or "crossbreeding."

## genderism

*n.* Discrimination based upon a person's sex.

Reported from 1984 (in the *Manchester Guardian Weekly*). Constructed by joining *gender*, meaning "sex," with the suffix -*ism* (as in *sexism, racism,* and *ageism*). *Genderism* arose in response to the need for a term less charged with emotion than the established term *sexism.*

## glasnost

*n.* **1.** A political policy of open discussion and tolerance of peaceful dissent in the Soviet Union.
**2.** A similar policy in other countries, such as Poland and China.
**3.** A similar policy in nonpolitical contexts, such as economics, education, or labor.

Recorded from 1986 (in *The Christian Science Monitor*). Borrowed from Russian *glasnost*. Only time will tell if *glasnost* and its derivatives (*glasnostic, glasnostician,* and *glasnostified*) will be fully incorporated into English.

The pronunciation of the word in English is only a rough approximation of the Russian. In Russian the stress is on the first syllable, and the vowel sounds like the *a* in *father*; the second syllable sounds something like "nust." In English the first vowel sounds like anything from the *a* in *glad* to the *a* in *father*. The vowel in the second syllable may sound in English like the *a* in *father* or the *o* in *ghost*. Ironically, it has become fashionable in Moscow to use the American pronunciation in order to sound hip or cosmopolitan.

## golden exile

*n. phr.* Guaranteed reception of a deposed ruler allowing him or her to live comfortably and in relative security in a foreign country.

Recorded from 1982 (in *Time* magazine). Constructed by combining *golden* (as in *golden handshake* and *golden parachute*) with *exile* (as in *self-exile* and *fellow exile*). Although recorded from 1982, *golden exile* did not become prominent until 1988.

## gridlock

*n.* **1.** A massive traffic jam in which vehicles are unable to move in a network of intersections.
**2.** Any similarly congestive situation, such as in speaking (*vocal gridlock*), a bureaucracy (*corporate gridlock*), or an electronic system (*telephone gridlock*).

Recorded from 1980 (in *The New York Times Magazine*). Constructed by joining *grid*, meaning "a pattern of intersecting lines," with *lock*, as in the expression "a lock of carriages in traffic." Perhaps influenced by *wedlock*. See the entry -LOCK.

**gridlock**

## hara-kiri swap

*n. phr.* A commercial trading of currencies which ends in a financial loss or only a very small profit, undertaken in an effort to attract new customers.

Recorded from 1984 (in *The Economist* and the *Japan Economic Journal*). Constructed by combining *hara-kiri*, meaning "suicide by disembowelment as practiced in Japan," with *swap*, meaning "an exchange." This is not a borrowing because *hara-kiri* has been a part of English and because it is an archaic word in Japanese; the modern Japanese term is *seppuku*.

## Hawking radiation

*n. phr.* The telltale particles which, in theory, escape the gravity of a black hole in space.

Recorded from 1982 (in *Science News* magazine). Constructed by combining Stephen *Hawking*, the name of the astrophysicist who theorized the existence of these particles, with *radiation* (as in *background radiation*).

## HIV

*n.* The virus that is commonly acknowledged to cause AIDS. *HIV* is a term preferred by

American scientists; European scientists often prefer *LAV* (lymphadenapathy virus). *HTLV* (human T-cell leukemia virus) is another synonym for the AIDS virus. So many varieties of the virus have been discovered that numbers are being added to the names to differentiate the viruses: *HIV-1, HIV-2, HTLV-I, HTLV-II, HTLV-III,* and *HTLV-IV.*

Recorded from 1986 (in *Scientific American* magazine). Constructed as an abbreviation of *human immunodeficiency virus. HIV* is now the internationally accepted term.

### hot bunk

*n.* A sailor's bunk bed shared on a rotation basis with other sailors.

Recorded from 1981 (in *The New York Times Magazine*). Constructed by combining *hot*, because the bed is in constant use, with *bunk.*

### hundredth-monkey phenomenon

*n. phr.* A controversial theory proposed as an explanation for the supposed spontaneous spread of behavior when a population of animals reaches a certain high number.

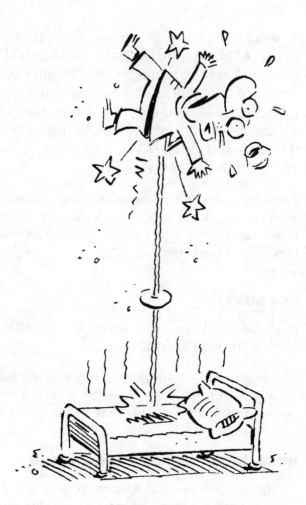

**hot bunk**

Recorded from 1979 (in *Lifetide: The Biology of the Unconscious*), but not common until 1985 (in the *National Review*). Constructed by combining *hundredth monkey*, because the hundredth monkey is supposed to have marked the threshold for the learning of sweet-potato washing, with *phenomenon* (as in *interference phenomenon*).

## image spill

*n.* A sudden accidental loss of credibility on the part of a public figure, especially of a candidate during a political campaign.

Recorded from 1983 (in *Time* magazine). Constructed by combining *image* (as in *public image*) with *spill* (as in *oil spill*).

## infobit

*n.* An individual item of information, such as a recipe or a description of a place, that meets the requirements for inclusion in a data bank.

Recorded from 1982 (in *Library Journal*). Constructed by joining *info-*, the clipped form of *information*, with *bit*, meaning "a small unit," as an intentional pun on the computer acronym *bit*, meaning "a binary digit."

## information literacy

*n. phr.* The ability to use and analyze sources of information efficiently.

Recorded from 1985 (in *PC Week*). Constructed by combining *information* (as in *information revolution*) with *literacy* (as in *computer literacy*). The term in its adjective form, *information-literate*, is recorded from 1984, which might justify speculation that the noun suffix, *-acy*, was substituted for the "original" adjective suffix, *-ate*.

## infomercial

*n.* Also spelled **informercial.** A television program that presents a demonstration or lengthy discussion of a product or service and is paid for by the manufacturer or provider of the service.

*Informercial* recorded from 1981 (in *The Christian Science Monitor*); *infomercial* recorded from 1984 (in the *Harvard Business Review*). Constructed by joining *info-*, the clipped form of *information*, with the clipped form of *commercial*, meaning "advertisement."

## jellies

*n. pl.* Also called **jelly bean shoes**. Rubber or flexible plastic shoes for casual wear by girls, characterized by a wide variety of colors.

Recorded from 1980 (in *Newsweek*). *Jellies* is constructed by the reduction of the phrase *jelly bean shoes*, which is a reference to the brightly colored candy. Perhaps influenced by *jellybean*, meaning "a flashy dresser."

## jogger's paw

*n. phr.* A condition among dogs accompanying joggers, in which the pads of the paws become sore or split.

Recorded from 1986 (in the *Chicago Tribune*). Constructed by combining *jogger* with *paw*. Patterned after *swimmer's ear, runner's knee,* and *surfer's knob.*

## joygerm fever

*n. phr.* A mental condition characterized by happiness, kindness, and courtesy.

Recorded from 1987 (in *The New York Times Magazine*). Constructed by combining *joygerm*, meaning "infectious happiness" (compare earlier *joy juice* for "liquor" and *joy ride*, as well as *disease germ*) with *fever* (as in *gold fever, spring fever,* and *cabin fever*).

## junk-food imperialism

*n. phr.* Aggressive international marketing of food that is high in calories but low in nutri-

**jogger's paw**

tional value, such as candy and most fast foods. Also called **fast-food imperialism**.

Recorded from 1984 (in the *Manchester Guardian Weekly*). Constructed by combining *junk food* with *imperialism* (as in *cultural imperialism*).

## Karmarkar's algorithm

*n. phr.* A technique of quickly solving a complex mathematical problem by eliminating groups of possible solutions with the aid of solid geometry.

Recorded from 1984 (in the *New Scientist*). Constructed by combining Dr. Narendra *Karmarkar*, the name of the Indian-born mathematician working for AT&T's Bell Laboratories who devised it, with *algorithm*, meaning "a set of rules for the solution of a mathematical problem in a finite number of steps" (as in *Euclid's algorithm* for finding the greatest common divisor).

## knucklecurve

*n.* A baseball pitch that causes the ball to drop abruptly just before reaching the batter.

Recorded from 1981 (in *The New York Times*). Constructed by combining the clipped form of *knuckleball* with *curve* (as in *curveball*).

### Lake Wobegon effect

*n. phr.* The paradoxical claim that all the students tested are above average in educational performance.

Reported from 1987 (on National Public Radio). Constructed by combining *Lake Wobegon,* the mythical town in Minnesota in the radio program "The Prairie Home Companion," "where the women are strong, the men are good looking, and all the children are above average," with *effect* (as in *ripple effect).* The Lake Wobegon effect was first noticed by Dr. John Cannell of West Virginia.

### language police

*n. phr.* The popular name in English for the commission in the Province of Quebec that is charged with enforcing the law making French the official language.

Recorded from 1982 (in the *Manchester Guardian Weekly*). Constructed by combining *language* (as in *language laboratory*) with *police* (as in *fire police*), probably patterned directly on *Thought Police* in George Orwell's novel *1984* (c. 1949).

### language pollution

*n. phr.* The use of many new expressions, slang terms, or foreign words, when viewed as either unnecessary or offensive.

**language police**

Recorded from 1981 (in *People's Daily* in an editorial summarized in the BBC *Summary of World Broadcasts*). Constructed by combining *language* (as in *language arts*) with *pollution* (as in *environmental pollution*). See also ELECTROPOLLUTION.

## laser-eyed

*adj.* **1.** having a piercingly aggressive expression.
**2.** sharp-eyed; paying thorough and careful attention to details.

Recorded from 1980 (in *The Washington Post*). Constructed from *laser* (as a figurative extension in *laser surgery*) with *-eyed* (as in *evil-eyed* or *eagle-eyed*).

## -lock

*Combining form.* Inability to move; paralysis; a jam. The words created with this word element are usually concocted with a humorous twist and are characteristically short-lived, such as *aqualock* (of a harbor), *boatlock, cablock* (of taxi traffic), and *pedlock* (of pedestrians).

Recorded from 1982 (in *The New York Times*). Formed as a clipping from GRIDLOCK, meaning "a gigantic traffic jam."

### low-jinks

*n.* Irreverent, obscene, or coarse pranks or jokes.

Recorded from 1980 (in *Newsweek*, in a review of Anne Tyler's novel *Morgan's Passing*). Constructed by substituting *low* (as in *low-grade* or *lowbrow*) for the *high* in *high-jinks*. Many of the occurrences of the word *low-jinks* appear in texts very close to the word *high-jinks*.

### lying-in-the-road death

*n. phr.* The accidental death of a pedestrian, caused by the drunkenness of the victim who falls asleep or faints in a rural roadway and is run over by an unsuspecting motorist.

Recorded from 1986 (in *The New York Times*). Constructed by combining *lying-in-the-road*, because it is this position the victim assumes, with *death* (as in *crib death*).

### megadebt

*n.* **1.** Commercial loans or government financial debt of unusually great magnitude.
**2.** Personal indebtedness that is financially crippling.

Recorded from 1983 (in *The New Republic*). Constructed by joining the combining form *mega-* (as in *megabucks* or *megadose*) with *debt* (as in *national debt*).

## megatrend

*n.* Also spelled **mega-trend**. A far-reaching or widespread change in society, such as the advent of computers and the information revolution, aerobics and physical fitness, microwave ovens, and convenience foods.

Recorded from 1983 (in *Computerworld*). Constructed by joining the combining form *mega-* (as in MEGADEBT) with *trend* (as in *downtrend* or *uptrend*). The word became widely known as the title of a book (c. 1982) by John Naisbitt about changes taking place in American society.

## memory hole

*n. phr.* Oblivion; state of being entirely forgotten; the obliteration of facts or the record of events and people to suit one's own desires.

Recorded from 1979 (in *U.S. News & World Report*). A generalizing of the nickname for the wastepaper disposal tubes at the Ministry of Truth in George Orwell's novel *1984* (c. 1949). See also LANGUAGE POLICE.

**memory hole**

## mercy rule

*n. phr.* A formula in baseball that allows for the shortening of a game when one team is so far behind in the score that catching up is highly unlikely.

Recorded from 1986 (in the *Los Angeles Times*). Constructed by combining *mercy* (as in *mercy killing* and *mercy stroke*) with *rule* (as in *ground rule[s]*).

## microburst

*n.* A sudden downdraft of the atmosphere associated with wind shear that disrupts the control of airplane traffic around airports.

Recorded from 1981 (in *Aviation Week and Space Technology*). Constructed by joining the combining form *micro-* (as in *microearthquake* or *microenvironment*) with *burst* (as in *outburst*).

## microwavable

*adj.* Also spelled **microwaveable**. Capable of being cooked or prepared in a microwave oven as opposed to a conventional oven.

Recorded from 1982 (in *The New York Times*). Constructed by joining *microwave* (as in *micro-*

*wave oven)* with the suffix *-able* (as in the much older manufacturing term *ovenable*).

## minibang

*n.* **1.** An explosion involving much smaller amounts of energy and matter than that of the big bang, thought to be the origin of the universe in its current state.
**2.** Any noteworthy event in the physical history of the universe.
**3.** An event in banking and finance of limited importance.

Recorded from 1981 (in *The Economist*). Constructed by joining the combining form *mini-* (as in *minirecession*) with *bang* (from *big bang*).

## narco-

*Combining form.* Involving or relying upon illegal drug dealing. This new word element is responsible for a number of new compounds, including: *narco-militarism, narco-military, narco-terror, narco-terrorism, narco-terrorist,* and *narco-traffic.*

Reported from 1984 (in *The Nation*). A shift in usage of the word *narco,* a noun meaning "a drug trafficker." Originally *narco* meant "a narcotics agent."

**minibang**

## neoism

*n.* An old policy or idea presented in a way that makes it appear new or innovative.

Recorded from 1982 (in *The Washington Post*). Constructed by joining the combining form *neo-* (as in *neologism* or *neoconservative*) with the suffix *-ism* (as in *yuppie-ism*).

## new-collar

*adj.* Of or having to do with a middle-class voter, worker, etc., who grew up in a blue-collar family as part of the baby-boom generation, especially a person who works in the service sector of the economy. See also BRIGHT COLLAR.

Recorded from 1981 (in *Newsweek*). Constructed by combining *new* (as in *new poor* or *new money*) with *collar* (as in *blue collar, white collar,* and *pink collar*).

## nonchaotic attractor

*n. phr.* A pattern of movement in a system with motion, such as a pendulum, that settles down to an easily describable and predictable pattern, unlike CHAOTIC ATTRACTOR.

Recorded from 1986 (in *Scientific American*). Constructed by joining *non-* (as in *nonperiodic*) with the term CHAOTIC ATTRACTOR.

## obligate runner

*n. phr.* A person who obsessively pursues physical fitness through a program of jogging, especially to the point of causing physical pain or injury.

Recorded from 1983 (in *The Washington Post*). Constructed by combining *obligate*, meaning "compulsive," with *runner* (as in *fun runner*).

The pronunciation of the first part of this term is AHB-li-guht.

## offenders' tag

*n. phr.* An electronic device worn by a person under house arrest that monitors his or her movements and alerts police to violations of restrictions of movement.

Recorded from 1985 (in *The Economist*). Constructed by combining *offender* (as in *offender status*) with *tag* (as in *dog tag*).

**obligate runner**

## optronics

*n.* The physics of mirrors, prisms, and lasers used in substituting light beams for electrical currents, as is being done in fiber optics.

Recorded from 1981 (in *Defense & Foreign Affairs*). Constructed by joining the clipped form of *optical* (as in *optical fiber*) with the clipped form of *electronics* (as in *mechatronics*).

## Oz

*n.* Australia or the English language as spoken in Australia.

*adj.* Australian.

Recorded from 1987 in American English (in *Connoisseur* magazine). Substitution of *Oz* for *Aus.*, the abbreviation of *Australia,* because their pronunciation in Australian English is the same, and because *Oz,* the city where the Wizard lived in Lyman Frank Baum's story *The Wonderful Wizard of Oz,* is portrayed as a far-off place of wonder and mystery.

## parapublic

*adj.* Having to do with both the private and public sectors of the economy at the same time or with people who work in both spheres.

Recorded from 1982 (in *Maclean's* magazine). Constructed by joining the combining form *para-* (as in *paragovernmental* or *parapolitical*) with *public* (as in *public service*).

## parking condo

*n. phr.* Space in a garage or parking lot that may be purchased for the storage of an automobile just as a person purchases an apartment condominium to live in.

Recorded from 1986 (in *Forbes* magazine). Constructed by combining *parking* (as in *parking lot*) with *condo,* the popular shortening for *condominium.*

## people meter

*n.* An electronic device that is attached to a television set for surveying the preferences of the television audience.

Recorded from 1984 (in *The New York Times*). Constructed by combining *people* (as in *people mover*) with *meter* (as in *applause meter* or *gas meter*).

## permaculture

*n.* An alternative life-style based on agriculture in which each of the related activities is

**people meter**

located to help conserve energy.

Recorded from 1985 (in *The New York Times*). Constructed by joining the clipped form of *permanent* (as in *permafrost*) with the clipped form of *agriculture* (as in *aboriculture*).

## phone accountant

*n. phr.* A monitoring device on a telephone that records the time, date, duration, and phone number of a telephone call.

Recorded from 1987 (in *The New York Times*). Constructed by combining *phone* (as in *phone call*) with *accountant* (as in *cost accountant*).

## pi wars

*n. phr.* The competition among computer experts to refine the value of the mathematical constant $\pi$, 3.14159 . . . , which is the number expressing the constant relationship of the diameter of any circle to its circumference.

Recorded from 1982 (in *Science News*). Constructed by combining *pi*, the mathematical constant, with *wars* (as in *Star Wars*).

## politicide

*n.* Political suicide; loss of power in politics by accepting a compromise.

Recorded from 1980 (in *The New York Times*). Constructed by joining the clipped form of *political* (as in *politicization*) with the combining form *-cide* (as in *liberticide* or *regicide*).

## post-preppie

*adj.* **1.** Of or having to do with someone who acts like a preppie but is too old to be a student or recent graduate of a preparatory school.
**2.** Having to do with the fashions that followed the craze for jackets, ties, sweaters, skirts, and blouses of the preppie look.
*n.* Someone considered too old to be thought of as a preparatory-school student.

Recorded from 1982 (in *Business Week*). Constructed by joining the prefix *post-* (as in *postgraduate*) with *preppie*, meaning "a preparatory-school student or the styles preppies prefer."

## pre-preppie

*adj.* Of or having to do with someone who acts like a preppie but is too young to be a preparatory-school student, especially a child who is not yet a teenager.

Recorded from 1985 (in the *Pittsburgh Business Times & Journal*). Constructed by joining the prefix *pre-* (as in *preadult*) with *preppie*, perhaps as a reaction to the earlier word POST-PREPPIE.

## proactive

*adj.* Of or having to do with an approach to changing situations in which people anticipate events and actively seek to influence them.

Recorded from 1984 (in *Computerworld*). Probably constructed by substituting the prefix *pro-* (as in *protective*) for the prefix *re-* (as in *reactive*). The earlier usage in psychology from the 1930s referring to "the interference from the lingering effects of conditions which preceded the learning" is unrelated.

## Qaddafism

*n.* Also called **Qaddafi-ism**. The polices and practices of Muammar Qaddafi, the political leader of Libya since 1969, especially his ardent religious fundamentalism and uncompromising opposition to Western culture.

Recorded from 1981 (in *The Washington Post*). Constructed by joining *Qaddafi,* the name of the ruler of Libya, with the suffix *-ism* (as in *McCarthyism* or *Stalinism*).

## quipstering

*adj.* Using clever or witty remarks in one's conversation or writing.

Recorded from 1982 (in *Maclean's* magazine). Constructed by joining *quipster* with the suffix *-ing,* the inflection that turns verbs into adjectives or nouns.

## racer chaser

*n.* **1.** A person hired by the manufacturer of skis to help contestants prepare and maintain their equipment, thereby improving their chances of a good performance.
**2.** Any person who follows the competitors in a sport from one competition to the next.

Recorded from 1983 (in *The New York Times*). Constructed by combining *racer* (as in *road racer*) with *chaser* (as in *ambulance chaser*).

## rap

*n.* Also called **rap music.** A style of rock music with a pronounced rhythmical beat and em-

**quipstering**

phasis upon the rhyme of the lyrics rather than upon the instrumental accompaniment.
*adj.* Of or having to do with rap.
*v.* To sing or play in the style of rap.

Recorded from 1980 (in *The Washington Post*). A shift of meaning from *rap*, meaning "conversation," a popular term of the 1970s, first recorded in the late 19th century.

## resource rape

*n.* The overtaxing of a large library's collection through the interlibrary loan system, so that the large library's staff is unable to serve its regular patrons effectively.

Recorded from 1986 (in *American Libraries* magazine). Constructed by combining *resource* (as in *resource recovery*) with *rape* (as in *statutory rape*).

## reverse vending

*n. phr.* The dispensing of money or credit slips for an item deposited in a machine, such as an empty bottle or can, as part of a campaign to recycle used containers.

Recorded from 1983 (in *The New York Times*). Constructed by combining *reverse* (as in *reverse psychology*) with *vending* (as in *vending machine*).

## reversible raincoat sentence

*n. phr.* A statement that with a minor change, as in word order or word substitution, produces a cleverly expressed idea, as in: "Ask not what your country can do for you; ask what you can do for your country."

Recorded from 1982 (in *The New York Times*). Constructed by combining *reversible raincoat*, because of its ability to be turned inside out, with *sentence,* because its word order is often all that is changed.

## revirginization

*n.* The reestablishment of a person's virginity, especially in the eyes of some Roman Catholics, thereby allowing that person to enter a holy order from which he or she would otherwise be excluded.

Recorded from 1982 (in *Maclean's* magazine). Constructed by joining the prefix *re-* (as in *requalify*) and the suffix *-ization* (as in *Latinization*) with the noun *virgin* (as in *vestal virgin*).

## roll

*n.* In the phrase **on a roll**. Experiencing a series of successful events or victories or a period of intense activity.

Recorded from 1980 (in *The Washington Post*). Perhaps constructed from *roll*, meaning "a roll of the dice." Probably influenced by such phrases as *on one's way, to roll along, get rolling,* and *get the ball rolling*. In the first half of the year 1980 all the references are to sports teams.

## scissor wing

*n. phr.* The wing of an aircraft that pivots forward on one side of the plane and backward on the other side in order to reduce wind resistance during high-speed flight.

Recorded from 1982 (in *High Technology* magazine). Constructed by combining *scissor* (as in *scissor-winged bird* or *scissor blade*) with *wing* (as in *swing-wing* or *delta wing*).

## sewergator

*n.* An alligator that lives in a municipal sewage system, especially when thought of as a pest.

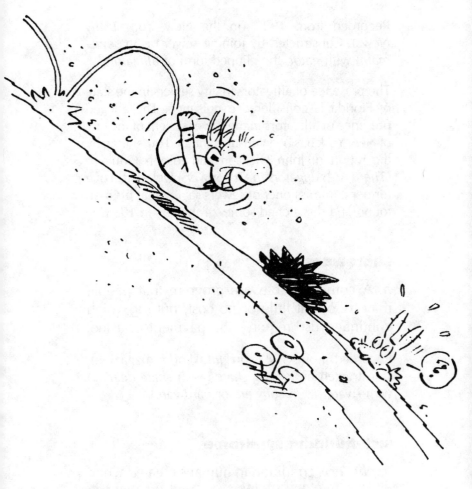

**roll**

Recorded from 1987 (in the New York *Daily News*). Constructed by joining *sewer* (as in *sewer main*) with *gator*, the clipped form of *alligator*.

The presence of alligators in city sewers in the state of Florida is considered a nuisance. The alleged presence of alligators in the sewer system of the city of New York has been unsubstantiated other than by the report of John Dickson and Joseph Goulden (*There Are Alligators in Our Sewers,* Delacorte) of a former commissioner of sewers saying that his men found and dispatched some 24-inchers in 1935.

## shareware

*n.* A computer software program that people may try out at little or no cost, but for which continued use requires the payment of a fee.

Recorded from 1983 (in *InfoWorld* magazine). Constructed by joining *share* (as in *share-dealing*) with *-ware* (as in *software* or *hardware*).

## sick-building syndrome

*n. phr.* **1.** A condition in humans created when a substance that pollutes the environment becomes trapped in a building, especially due to poor design or hazardous materials being used in construction. Sometimes called **tight-building syndrome.**

**sick-building syndrome**

**2.** Any building design that contributes to a condition of illness in humans.

Recorded from 1983 (in *Industry Week*). Constructed by combining *sick-building* (compare *sick child*) with *syndrome* (as in *battered-baby syndrome*).

## smartcard

*n.* A bank card, credit card, or similar plastic card featuring a computer microchip or a hologram that contains fingerprints, a voiceprint, information about one's credit and health, etc.

Recorded from 1980 (in *American Banker* magazine). Constructed by joining *smart* (as in *smart bomb*) with *card* (as in *credit card* or *donor card*).

## sniglet

*n.* A made-up word for something without a name or concise description, based upon a pun or a clever combination of existing words.

Recorded from 1983 (in *The New York Times*). Constructed by joining the clipped form of *sniggle*, meaning "a snicker," with the suffix *-let* (as in *droplet* or *caplet*). The term has been popularized in the title of a series of books containing such humorous concoctions by Richard Hall, a writer and actor.

## snowboard

*n.* A single wide ski that resembles a short, narrow surfboard, for riding down ski slopes.

Recorded from 1985 (in *The Washington Post*). Constructed by joining *snow* (as in *snowshoe*) with *board*, the clipped form of *surfboard*. No doubt this is an invention independent of the earlier word *snowboard*, meaning "a deflector of snow sliding down a mountainside."

## Snuba

*n.* A system for supplying air to underwater swimmers from a raft at the surface through a long tube so that swimmers do not have to stay near the surface or wear bulky air tanks. A trademark.

Recorded from 1988 (in *Time* magazine). Constructed by joining the clipped form of *snorkel*, meaning "a tube for a swimmer to breathe through while swimming at the surface," with the clipped form of *scuba*, an acronym for "self-contained underwater breathing apparatus."

## space barrel

*n. phr.* Legislation appropriating money to space exploration that benefits a small group of

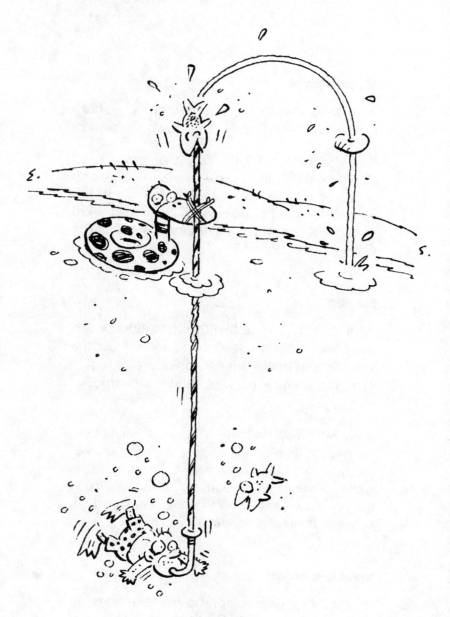

**Snuba**

people, especially through the assignment of government contracts.

Recorded from 1985 (in *Time* magazine). Constructed by combining *space* (as in *space program*) with (pork) *barrel.*

## spin

*n.* **1.** Influence or bias, especially in the interpretation of statements at a news conference by a politician.
**2.** Especially in the phrase: **put a** (positive, negative, etc.) **spin on** (something), meaning "to give a (positive or negative) interpretation or bias to."
**3.** *Used attributively* as in **spin control,** meaning "the effort to direct spin," and **spin doctor,** meaning "one who attempts to control spin."

Recorded from 1984 (in *The Atlantic*). A shift in meaning by the metaphorical use of *spin* (as in *put spin on the ball*).

## substellar

*adj.* **1.** Having too little mass to be classified as a star.
**2.** Of, or having to do with, theatrical acting not worthy of a star.

Recorded from 1984 (in *The New York Times*). Constructed by joining the prefix *sub-* (as in *sublethal*) with *stellar*.

## supergridlock

*n.* A gigantic traffic jam extending over many miles, especially beyond the limits of a single city.

Recorded from 1981 (in *The New York Times*). Constructed by joining the prefix *super-* (as in *supertax*) with GRIDLOCK.

## techno-hip

*adj.* Comfortable with the use of the modern jargon of computers and of other recent technological developments.

Recorded from 1987 (in *Discover*). Constructed by joining *techno-* (as in *technostress*) with *hip*, meaning "understanding modern ways."

## telebridge

*n.* A two-way television link, especially by satellite relay between audiences in distant nations.

Recorded from 1984, in English (in the BBC *Summary of World Broadcasts,* as the English text of a Moscow news conference, later in *The Christian Science Monitor*). Borrowed from Russian *telemost* (*Pravda,* 1965) with the translation of *most,* meaning "bridge." Because *tele-* is a combining form shared by Russian and English, *telemost* became a prime candidate for translation.

### three o'clock syndrome

*n. phr.* **1.** The tendency of office employees to become drowsy in the midafternoon.
**2.** The tendency on the part of working mothers to feel guilty about being away from home when their children arrive there from school.

Recorded from 1980 (in *Maclean's* magazine). Constructed by combining *three o'clock* (as in *three o'clock meeting*) with *syndrome* (as in *retirement syndrome*).

### thrust bucket

*n.* **1.** The brief reduction in forward thrust of a rocket engine before passing through the sound barrier in order to reduce the dangerous stresses on the craft.
**2.** The mechanism in a jet engine for briefly reversing the thrust as an aid to braking an airplane after landing.

**three o'clock syndrome**

Recorded from 1980 (in *Aviation Week and Space Technology*). Constructed by combining *thrust* (as in *thrust chamber*) with *bucket* (as in *plunger bucket*).

## Thucydides syndrome

*n. phr.* A disease that resembles flu but which is complicated by toxic-shock syndrome. Its symptoms closely resemble the plague of ancient Athens, which Thucydides described from personal experience as high fever, inflammation of the eyes and throat, inflamed skin, and severe diarrhea.

Recorded from 1985 (in *The Washington Post*). Constructed by combining *Thucydides,* the Greek historian who lived in the 5th century B.C., with *syndrome* (as in *Down's syndrome*).

## tin parachute

*n. phr.* Salary and benefits guaranteed to non-management employees when the control of a business is transferred to new owners.

Recorded from 1987 (in *Dun's Business Month*). Constructed by substituting *tin* (as in *tin ear*) for the first word in the phrase *golden parachute*, meaning "salary and benefits guaranteed to management employees when a business is transferred to new owners." *Golden parachute* is probably based upon *golden handshake* from the 1960s; the choice of *parachute* was perhaps influenced by *What Color Is Your Parachute? A Practical Manual for Job-Hunters and Career Changers*, ©1982.

## toxic tort

*n. phr.* Harm or injury caused by environmental pollution for which the injured person has a right to sue for damages in a court of law.

Recorded from 1980 (in *Fortune* magazine). Constructed by combining *toxic* (as in *toxic-shock syndrome*) with *tort* (as in *intentional tort*).

## transformable plush

*n. phr.* A doll having an exterior fabric with a long nap that is capable of being reshaped into a dramatically different form.

Recorded from 1985 (in *Chain Store Age* and later in *Advertising Age*). Constructed by combining *transformable* (as in *transformable quality*) with *plush* (as in *cotton plush*). The popularity of the toy robots dubbed Transformers may have influenced the choice of *transformable*.

## triple witching hour

*n. phr.* The final hour of trading in stock options, stock-index futures, and stock-index options when these contracts expire on the third Friday of a calendar quarter.

Recorded from 1985 (in *Business Week*). Constructed by combining *triple* (as in *triple somersault*), because three financial instruments are involved, with *witching hour,* meaning "a time when witches are about."

## 'tweener

*n.* Also written **tweener**. **1.** A ballplayer who is too small for one position and either too big or not good enough for another position.
**2.** A yuppie who maintains contact with the people of his or her nonprofessional roots.

Recorded from 1978 (in *The Washington Post*). Constructed by clipping off the initial syllable of *between. Between* comes from Old English *be-,* meaning "by," joined with *tweon*, a form of *twa,* meaning "two."

## 20th-century syndrome

*n. phr.* Also called **20th-century disease**. Any collection of disease symptoms attributable to developments of this century, such as *toxic-shock syndrome,* SICK-BUILDING SYNDROME, and *Munich syndrome.*

Recorded from 1983 (in *The Washington Post*). Constructed by combining *20th century* (as in *20th-century cut,* of a diamond) with *syndrome* (as in THUCYDIDES SYNDROME).

## user-friendly

*adj.* **1.** Easy to use with a computer, especially applied to a software program that prompts the user, combines operations, or otherwise simplifies the user's task.
**2.** Easy to understand, such as the design of an airport, information on product labels, or the operation of home appliances.

Recorded from 1980 (in *The Christian Science Monitor,* earlier in technical reports). Constructed by combining *user* (as in *user group* or *user fee*) with *friendly* (as in *superfriendly*).

## U-turn worker

*n. phr.* A professional or skilled worker who returns from employment in a big city to work in the nonurban locality from which he or she came.

Recorded from 1985 (in *New Scientist*). Perhaps a loan translation from Japanese; compare *yū-tān* (a Japanese adaptation of the English word *U-turn*)

**user-friendly**

and *hataraki-,* meaning "worker" (as in *hataraki-ari,* a worker ant).

## Uzi

*n.* **1.** Any brand of automatic assault rifle resembling that developed for the Israeli army. **2.** Anything which is similarly potent, aggressive, or overpowering, such as bad breath being described as *uzi-breath.*
*v.* To use an automatic assault rifle on (someone).

Recorded from 1989 (in *The Boston Globe*). A shift of meaning from the name of the first such assault rifle, which was constructed by clipping the name of *Uziel Gal,* the Israeli designer of the assault rifle.

## vaporware

*n.* Computer software that has been proposed but never commercially distributed.

Recorded from 1984 (in *Computerworld* magazine). Constructed by joining *vapor* (as in *vaporturbaned*), because it is as intangible as vapor, with *-ware* (as in *software* and *hardware*). See also SHAREWARE.

## video visit

*n. phr.* **1.** A videotape recording of family members or friends sent to another person as a recorded message, especially to an older relative in a nursing home.
**2.** A videotape recording of a conversation between two people together.

Recorded from 1985 (in *The Washington Post*). Constructed by combining *video* (as in *videocassette*) with *visit* (as in *social visit*).

## voice lineup

*n. phr.* A selection of voices, usually recorded, presented one at a time to the victim of a crime who is asked to identify a suspect.

Recorded from 1979 (in *The Washington Post*). Constructed by combining *voice* (as in *voiceprint*) with *lineup* (as in *police lineup*). This term did not become common until 1988.

## vulture capitalist

*n. phr.* A person who invests money in a risky project, usually in the form of a loan unsecured by collateral, in return for a very high rate of interest.

**vulture capitalist**

Recorded from 1978 (in *The Washington Post*). Constructed by combining *vulture* (as in the metaphorical sense of "an unscrupulous businessman") with *capitalist* (as in *venture capitalist*).

## windshield appraisal

*n. phr.* A very superficial inspection of collateral by a lender, especially of a house of an applicant for a home-improvement loan.

Recorded from 1986 (in *Commercial Lending Review,* later in *American Banker*). Constructed by combining *windshield* (as in *windshield wiper*) with *appraisal,* because the appraiser looks at the house through the window of a car as he or she drives by.

## wogging

*n.* Jogging interspersed with periods of walking at a brisk pace, especially as a form of aerobic exercise.

Recorded from 1981 (in *The New York Times Book Review*). Constructed by blending *w*(alking) with (j)*ogging.*

## workaphile

*n.* A person who appears to be a workaholic but who is motivated by enjoyment in the task rather than by a compulsive desire to work.

Recorded from 1985 (in *The Bulletin*, from Australia). Constructed by joining *work* (as in *work ethic*) with the combining form *-phile* (as in *cyberphile* and *cinephile*).

## workquake

*n.* An upheaval in the way workers pursue their assignments in the workplace, especially as a result of computerization.

Recorded from 1982 (in *Maclean's* magazine). Constructed by joining *work* (as in *workplace*) with *quake* (as in *earthquake* or *seaquake*).

## X/Open

*n.* A group of computer companies that is seeking to develop an internationally accepted standard for different computers all of which use Unix, the disk operating system developed by AT&T in competition with the disk operating systems for IBM and Digital Research Corp.

Recorded from 1985 (in *Datamation* magazine). Constructed by combining *x*, in *Unix*, with *open*, from the formal name of the group: *Open Group for Unix Systems.*

## young fogy

*n. phr.* A young person who is as conventional as an old fogy; a very conservative young person. Also written **young fogey.**

Recorded from 1985 (in *The Times*, from London). Constructed by substituting *young* (as in *young Turk*) for the first word in the phrase *old fogy.*

## zap-proof

*adj.* Difficult to interrupt or blank out, as ads or other unwanted portions of a television program when making a videotape recording.

Recorded from 1985 (in *Ad Day* magazine). Constructed by combining *zap*, meaning "the blanking out of unwanted portions of a television program when taping it," with the combining form *-proof* (as in *soundproof* or *recessionproof*).